Gardeners'
Worldmagazine

101 Bold and
Beautiful Flowers

10 9 8 7 6 5 4 3 2

Published in 2008 by BBC Books,
an imprint of Ebury Publishing
A Random House Group Company

The Random House Group Limited Reg. No. 954009

Addresses for companies within the Random House Group can be
found at www.randomhouse.co.uk

A CIP catalogue record for this book is available from the British Library.

The Random House Group Limited supports The Forest Stewardship
Council (FSC), the leading international forest certification organization.
All our titles that are printed on Greenpeace approved FSC certified
paper carry the FSC logo. Our paper procurement policy can be found
at www.rbooks.co.uk/environment

To buy books by your favourite authors and register for offers visit
www.rbooks.co.uk

Printed and bound by Firmengruppe APPL, aprinta druck,
Wemding, Germany
Colour origination by GRB Editrice Ltd., London

Commissioning Editor: Lorna Russell
Project Editor: Laura Higginson
Designer: Kathryn Gammon
Production: Bridget Fish
ISBN: 9781846074479

Gardeners' World magazine

101 Bold and Beautiful Flowers

IDEAS FOR YEAR-ROUND COLOUR

Author
James Alexander-Sinclair

Picture researcher
Janet Johnson

Contents

Introduction

Imagine, if you would, an existence without flowers. It would be a joyless world; one with fewer surprises, without unexpected wafts of scent, without bouquets, without romance, without bees or butterflies and, above all, without colour. Everything would look like a rather depressing black-and-white television documentary.

Fortunately we are not in that position, and every day of every year some plant somewhere is flowering its little head off for our pleasure – maybe not in your garden, but in your street, a nearby park, a woodland or a hedgerow.

Flowers have the power to lift the spirits and soothe a troubled soul. We at *Gardeners' World Magazine* believe that the best medicine for anyone – young or old, with or without a garden – is to grow bright, colourful flowers. So in this book we suggest 101 ways in which you can bring bold and beautiful blooms into your life.

So read on, then find a pot or a patch of ground, sow a seed and as it grows and flowers, let it light up your life and the lives of all around you.

James Alexander-Sinclair
Gardeners' World Magazine

Don't miss James's celebration of favourite flowers in *Gardeners' World Magazine* every month.

Gardening terms made easy/jargon-buster

Gardening is a pretty easy hobby, but sometimes there are complicated terms for things that, once explained, are pretty straightforward. So we've come up with a handy glossary to help you make sense of some of the trickier gardening terms. If you can't find the word or phrase you're looking for visit www.gardenersworld.com and check out our online glossary.

Annual – a plant that completes its life cycle within one growing season.

Aphid – plant-feeding insects that are commonly known as greenfly, blackfly or plant lice.

Basal cutting – a cutting taken from fresh growth at the base of a plant (at ground level).

Deadheading – removing dead flowerheads from plants in order to encourage fresh blooms.

Divide, or division – a method of increasing your stock of herbaceous plants, by which the rootstock is split into smaller parts so that each one can be replanted as a new plant.

Germination – when a seed grows and sprouts above ground to become a seedling.

Half-hardy plants – plants that may be grown outdoors in summer, but which won't survive winter frosts in the garden.

Hardening off – the process of acclimatising plants to lower temperatures (useful for plants that have been started off under cover prior to planting them outside in open ground).

Hardwood cutting – a cutting taken from the wood (stems) of a plant when it is dormant (not in growth).

Hardy plants – plants able to withstand temperatures below 7°C (44°F).

Humus – decomposed organic matter that provides nutrients for plants and increases the soil's ability to retain water.

Hybrid – the plant that results from the cross-fertilisation of two or more plant species or genera.

Loam – rich, fertile soil composed from a balance of sand, clay and humus.

Mildew – a fungus that causes a powdery coating on the surfaces of affected plants. It occurs where plants have been exposed to damp conditions and can be prevented by good ventilation.

Mulch – a protective soil covering used to conserve moisture and suppress weeds. It can be organic (with leaves, bark, manure or compost) or inorganic (with pebbles or black plastic sheeting).

Naturalising – random planting (usually of bulbs, especially daffodils, in grass) to give the impression of naturally occurring plants.

Organic matter – rotted-down plant material that is rich in nutrients and is used to improve soil.

Perennial – a plant that lives for more than two years or three seasons. Flowering annually, these plants tend to die down during winter and return in spring.

Propagation – the processes of creating new plants by methods including grafting, division, cuttings, seed-sowing, budding and layering.

Rhizome – a creeping stem that grows along, or just beneath, the soil surface and has roots growing from it.

Root cutting – a way of propagating plants that produce shoots, or suckers, from their roots.

Semi-ripe cutting – a cutting that is taken when stems are firm and buds have developed.

Softwood cutting – a cutting taken from fresh, lush growth, usually in spring.

Sucker – a shoot arising from the base of a plant that will produce a new plant.

Tender – plants that are unable to withstand freezing temperatures.

Tilth – the fine, loose surface layer of soil that results from digging and raking the ground.

Tuber – a fleshy root or underground stem from which new growth develops.

Snapdragon
Antirrhinum majus 'Night and Day'

A colourful annual with reddish foliage, ideal for bedding or pots

Flowering time: July–October

To a child these plants hold almost as much fascination as feeding flies to Venus flytraps. The flower resembles the rearing head of a dragon, and if you squeeze each side of it the dragon's mouth opens and closes. Not exactly a snap, more of a toothless chomp, but still fascinating to a four-year-old – and it could be the starting point for a lifetime's passion for gardening. If you are going to plant snapdragons then plant plenty – there's nothing more dramatic than the sight of a sea of blood red lapping around the feet of shrubs in a mixed border or lots and lots in pots. In the official Royal Horticultural Society guide this plant is described as having a 'hairy palate', which is perhaps not something one would wish upon anybody.

Sow seed under glass any time from August to April. Even if they survive the winter (which they can in some sheltered places), it is best to start again each year with new plants.

Canna
Canna pfitzer 'Salmon Pink'

Exotic-looking tender perennial

Flowering time: July–October

Cannas tend to satisfy the longing for the tropics that many of us have. As we Brits sit at home in August watching the rain lash down on our gardens and ruin the barbecues we had planned, we can at least take a little comfort from the fact that in any short, sunny interval we can admire the majestic, slightly purple leaves of these plants. It is this dramatic foliage that takes us away to a distant land of dense jungle, skittering macaws and ripe paw-paws falling from the trees.

This canna, 'Salmon Pink', has very large pink flowers that tumble from reddish buds. Only growing to about 1m (3½ft) high (there are other, taller, varieties as well), it is best planted en masse with other equally exotic plants, such as ginger lilies (*Hedychium*) bananas (*Musa basjoo*) or hardy palm trees.

Rhizomes should be dug up after the first frosts and stored under cover. You can propagate from these by cutting them into short sections in spring, ensuring that each piece has a decent bud.

Pinks
Dianthus 'Lady in Red'

An old-fashioned, but perennially effective edging plant

Flowering time: June–July

Rather like the Chris de Burgh song of the same name, the dianthus is a bit out of fashion. It has been in our gardens for ages (in a seventeenth-century book John Parkinson lists over sixty different garden species), but for some reason it seems to have slipped out of favour. It will be back, though, because its delicate grey foliage and flamboyantly frilled petals make it irresistible.

Pinks come in so many colours that everybody can find one to love (although, as always happens with plants that are easy to hybridise, there are also some pretty hideous confections out there). But their best point is their scent; a mixture of clove and honeycomb with just a splash of lemon.

Get one you really like and you can easily propagate it by removing non-flowering shoots in summer and potting them into good-quality, well-drained compost. Deadhead regularly to prevent plants becoming straggly and to ensure long flowering.

Gloxinia
Gloxinia 'Glory Mixed'

Very colourful, summer-flowering conservatory plant

Flowering time: July–October

It is always a little alarming to see such a striking flower at quite such close quarters. Viewed from a few feet above, the gloxinia is startling, but it is only by getting up close and personal that we understand the full glories of any plant.

The velvet red of this gloxinia is the colour and texture of one of Violet Elisabeth Bott's (you remember Miss Bott – from the Just William stories) more eye-catching party dresses, with ruffled white edges to each petal. In the centre the stamens twist like a lightbulb filament – as if this flower needed to be any brighter. The leaves are dark, bluey-green and feel very slightly fuzzy to the touch.

Gloxinias are very tender, so they are really only suitable for growing in pots kept in a greenhouse or conservatory. Water them freely during the growing season and let them dry off in autumn. Keep out of direct sunlight in summer.

Scabious
Knautia macedonica 'Crimson Cushion'

A long-lasting, Caucasian scabious

Flowering time: June–October

This plant is like the perfect boyfriend and ticks all the right boxes. He will be polite and charming to your mother; he is immaculately turned out with deep burgundy, button flowers and narrow pea-green leaves; he is strong growing and only occasionally needs physical support, and his flowers are long-lasting, not at all smelly, unfailingly generous and never, ever late. Even better, when it is all over there are no recriminations and flying crockery, instead he fades gently away.

As the red petals fall like heartbroken tears, a beautiful, frog-green seedhead is revealed. *Knautia macedonica* 'Crimson Cushion' is fully hardy so it will last as long as you want it to, and because it reaches about 72cm (28in) high, it is invaluable in any mixed border. There are hardly any disadvantages to growing this plant – unless you are terribly jealous and possessive, as it is highly attractive to bees.

In good soil this plant will self-seed abundantly, but if it doesn't you can propagate from basal cuttings or sow seed in spring.

Oriental poppy
Papaver orientale 'Türkenlouis'

A strong-growing, perennial poppy perfect for early summer borders

Flowering time: May

This is one of the most exciting of the oriental poppies. I know it might seem a bit sad to get over-agitated about a poppy, but just look at it: an enormous, smiling-face that's about the size of a bright red saucer. Not just any red, but a red that is the colour of a Beefeater's waistcoat or the throbbing breast of a lovesick robin.

Amongst all this rubicund extravagance is a dark centre that is surrounded by a tight wig of black stamens. And then, just when you thought your heart would burst, it comes to your rapt attention that each perfect petal of this plant is fringed like the shawl of a fortune-teller. Aaaaah.

Oriental poppies will sprout easily from root cuttings: just trim off pieces of fleshy root each about the thickness of a pencil and cut into 5cm (2in) lengths, then pot them up.

Rose
Rosa 'Peter Beales'

A new, modern shrub rose that is perfect for the smaller garden

Flowering time: June–September

If you were ever to find yourself hang-gliding at dusk across the mouth of a volcano and happened to look down, then the sight that greeted you would be very similar to that of this flower. It has a crinoline of slightly ragged, velvet petals that are the colour of bubbling scarlet sunsets surrounding a glowing halo of molten gold.

'Peter Beales' is a short rose – reaching only about 90cm (3ft) high – so it is best grown in a container or as a low hedge, but what it lacks in stature it makes up for in attitude. It has a deep, fruity scent and an incredibly long flowering time. This rose was discovered in America only a few years ago and is named after the great Norfolk rose grower.

Roses are easier to propagate than you might think; they will not come true from seed, but they will grow easily from healthy hardwood cuttings taken in late autumn.

Sage
Salvia elegans 'Tangerine'

A very late-flowering, shrubby sage

Flowering time: September–October

It may seem a little strange that a plant whose striking flowers are, in anybody's book, as red as traffic lights managed to be named after an orange. Perhaps the plant breeder was colour-blind, or a little unfamiliar with some members of the citrus family?

The flowers of *Salvia elegans* 'Tangerine' are the shape of long, fanfaring trumpets – closer to bananas than tangerines. But pick a leaf, crush it and there is a distinct orangey scent (rather like the better-known pineapple sage).

In colder areas this 90cm (3ft) high shrub may never flower as it needs a lot of sunshine, in which case you may have to be satisfied with the leaves. That said, these leaves add a bit of extra texture and scent to fruit salads and cocktails.

This salvia is tender, so to avoid losing such a spectacular plant, bring it undercover in winter and take semi-ripe cuttings in autumn.

Begonia
Begonia 'Jessica'

An exotic, sub-tropical native widely used as a bedding plant

Flowering time: June–October

The unfortunate begonia seems to get more bad press than any other bedding plant (except, perhaps, the busy Lizzie). They are something that you will never see in a garden at the Chelsea Flower Show – so why is this?

For the prosecution: some of the available colours are revolting and occasionally the shape is more like one of those dolls used to cover lavatory rolls than a normal flower. For the defence: they are one of the few annuals that do not mind a bit of shade (indeed, they should be planted out of direct sunshine), and some are a perfectly delightful colour – such as Jessica, which is reminiscent of a lively orange sorbet. The leaves are also often interestingly spotted or marked, and sit beneath flowers that bloom unceasingly all summer.

These plants are mostly grown from tubers or ripe seed sown in spring, but they can also be propagated from the leaf, tip, basal or leaf cuttings, once established.

Marigold
Calendula officinalis 'Indian Prince'

An easy annual that will grow pretty well anywhere given some sun

Flowering time: June–September

This is a marigold – not one of those commonplace marigolds that we all grew as children, but an altogether rather superior sort of marigold. *Calendula officinalis* 'Indian Prince' has the sort of perfectly constructed and tastefully coloured flower that would make a fantastic skirt that could be worn by a lithe, bottom-shaking samba dancer shimmying her way along a hot boulevard in Brazil. It has dark, orange-yellow flowers with delicately feathered tips and flushed red undersides.

It will tolerate poor soils and so, supported by sturdy stems, makes a perfect edging to a path. It also works brilliantly among salad crops; not just for the colour but also because it attracts hoverflies – those stripy insects whose larvae crunch aphids by the dozen.

Either sow under glass in February or outside where it is to grow between March and May. To get really strong plants, try sowing outside in September. Deadhead regularly to extend its flowering season.

Ginger lily
Hedychium densiflorum 'Assam'

A taste of the primeval forest: big leaves and sweetly scented flowers

Flowering time: July–August

In a small garden it is often exciting to plant big things rather than lots of itsy-bitsy plants, and if this is how you feel, try a few exotic plants with big leaves and tall stems to create your own suburban jungle.

Ginger lily is one of the best plants to use if you are looking for that exotic, grass-skirted, doe-eyed, Pacific-islander look. The large leaves first appear in tight rolls before unfurling in early summer, then the densely packed flowers (hence the name – *densiflorum*) rocket up in late summer to stand like flamboyant bullrushes about 75cm (30in) above the leaves. The flowers, leaves and roots all smell deliciously of ginger.

Ginger lily will be fine in sheltered areas, but it does need a thick mulch over its roots if there is a danger of heavy frost.

The rhizomes can be easily split in spring to make new plants. Cut off a healthy piece with good roots and replant in a pot of compost.

Red hot poker
Kniphofia 'Nancy's Red'

A brightly coloured perennial that stands out in a border

Flowering time: June–September

All reds and oranges make very strong statements: not for them the pastel foothills of pink and mauve. Any gardener brave enough to use strong colours is a gardener who is unafraid of standing out from the crowd.

Of these strong tones, very few have the almost fluorescent quality that *Kniphofia multiflora* 'Nancy's Red' has in bundles. It glows right into the autumn like a marker buoy in a storm: a coral-reef red that is impossible to ignore. It is not a tall plant – reaching only about 60cm (2ft) high – but it is easily capable of holding its own among grasses and late summer daisies (especially low rudbeckias and *Aster cordifolius*). The leaves are soft green and sword-shaped.

For the best results, grow it in deep, fertile soil and divide congested clumps in spring. In frosty areas, mulch young plants with straw or leaves for the first year, until they have toughened up a bit.

Pelargonium
Pelargonium 'Horizon Orange'

A South African native that is great for vibrant summer colour

Flowering time: April–September

A pelargonium is what many people call a geranium – although, if you wish to be totally correct, a geranium is actually an herbaceous plant that is best placed at the front of borders and there is no family connection at all.

Pelargoniums look their best when planted in containers – I think they look a bit out of place anywhere else. There are varieties that trail, varieties with lots of leaf, varieties with huge flowers, varieties with scented leaves and varieties of different heights, all range from 20cm–45cm (8in–18in).

Pelargonium 'Horizon Orange' is an unusual orange (most of them are pinks, reds and white), being the colour of tinned tomato soup, and its flowers are clustered atop elegant stems and held above slightly fuzzy, waterlily-shaped leaves.

Pelargoniums will survive the winter if kept in a frost-free shed or greenhouse, but, to be absolutely safe, you could take cuttings for new plants any time from April to October.

Rose
Rosa 'Salvation'

A beautifully scented rose in an unusual colour

Flowering time: June–August

It may seem a slightly weird comparison, but this rose is reminiscent of a very complicated and intricately constructed piece of machinery. Look at the centre of the flower and imagine it as the epicentre of a gleaming turbine with perfectly engineered blades. The similarities end there, though, as no self-respecting machine is going to be seen in this colour; it is the sort of gingery-cream that is often foisted upon bridesmaids at a cousin's wedding. Unfortunate for them but rather glorious in a rose. The gentle colour of *Rosa* 'Salvation' makes a particularly stunning contrast with dark blue geraniums, such as 'Buxton's Blue'.

Named after the Salvation Army, this rose is a smallish shrub that reaches only about 82cm (32in) tall, so it is best planted towards the front of a border. Deadhead regularly to ensure consecutive flowering throughout the season.

Tulip
Tulipa 'Ballerina'

A stunning, powerfully coloured tulip

Flowering time: April

There is something particularly miraculous about bulbs; the magic starts in autumn when you get this smooth, solid lump that sits heavily in your palm and seems about as lively as a pebble. You dig a hole, put the bulb in and wait and then, six months later, that lump has transformed itself into something staggeringly beautiful.

No other plant is as satisfying to grow as this lily-flowered tulip – so-called because of the extraordinarily elegant curve and sway to its petals. This is a real 'wake up, spring is here' colour: streaked oscillating orange it sends a jolt through the spleen. Plant these bulbs in great drifts for a really dramatic effect: no matter how small your garden you should never buy less than fifty.

Success with tulips is easy the first year but, unless the drainage is perfect and you are prepared to lift them each year, storing them and keeping them dry in summer when dormant, they will lose vigour – so keep adding more.

Zinnia
Zinnia elegans 'Early Wonder'

One of a large family of many-coloured annuals

Flowering time: July–October

A real hangover cure, it will scour the eyeballs and overwork the cerebral flippers. The blooms of zinnia are very simple flowers that can often look as if they have been put together very carefully by a diligent child. Look closely and you can see the layers of petals are in perfect proportion with the largest and widest on the outside, the smallest and narrowest in the centre. The central stamens are like tiny, golden stars. All in all, it is a beautifully put-together flower – and the leaves aren't bad either.

Zinnia flowers are fantastic for cutting as a vase full will always cheer up a room. *Zinnia elegans* 'Early Wonder' is, as the name suggests, early flowering.

Zinnias are sometimes thought to be difficult to grow, but they aren't. They do, however, resent root disturbance so always sow seeds directly in the ground where you want them to flower. Do not overwater zinnias and be sure to pick them regularly, then they will flower until winter.

Yarrow
Achillea 'Walther Funcke'

A finely textured perennial for mid-season interest

Flowering time: June–August

A wonderful plant from an indispensable family. The leaves of this achillea are a slightly silver-green with finely cut, filigree edges, and the plate-shaped flowers go through a very expressive colour spectrum as they age. The young flowers are the colour of mellow red Tudor brickwork before fading through a dusky washed mandarin (the fruit, not the oriental potentate) ending up as a sort of anaemic, yellowing pink.

Achillea 'Walther Funcke' is a sensational plant when planted en masse, especially alongside *Stipa tenuissima* (a grass with the waviness and texture of a small child's hair) and anything with a strong, vertical flower spike, such as *Perovskia* 'Blue Spire'. It stands about 50cm (20in) high and shouldn't need staking.

Ensuring the plant has good drainage in winter is essential for long life. Dividing the plant in spring or autumn will help it to maintain vigour, while also providing new plants. Regular deadheading will increase its flowering time.

Siberian wallflower
Erysimum x *marshallii* 'Apricot Delight'

A beautifully scented, early flowering bedding plant

Flowering time: spring–summer

Wallflowers were the titans of the world of spring bedding throughout most of the last century, but sadly their stars began to wane and, according to the Royal Horticultural Society, the number of available cultivars slumped from nearly fifty to only about six a few years ago.

This collapse seemingly occurred through overuse and their appearance in some rather ropey public planting schemes. However, a renaissance is underway at last, especially for exciting varieties such as 'Apricot Delight'. The flowers are the colour of shredded carrot and go perfectly with beetroot-coloured tulips.

Buy plants as bare roots in autumn, but to be sure of getting the right variety, sow seed in July or August and move the plants to their flowering positions in November.

Sneezeweed
Helenium 'Rauchtopas'

A perky, late-flowering, strong-coloured perennial

Flowering time: June–September

Sneezeweed is a cheery fellow who saunters onto the scene at the end of June and proceeds to hang around at the back of a fertile border jollying things along – especially when other plants begin to flag. He will carry on flowering until August, growing to about 90cm (3ft) high. The flowers are daisy shaped, in the reddish buff of burnt toffee, while the dark brown centre of each flower could be a chocolate-covered caramel Rolo.

Helenium 'Rauchtopas' is a thoroughly amenable and trustworthy late-summer perennial that mingles easily with grasses, and particularly well with yellow rudbeckias. It is invaluable for livening up those exhausted spaces where early summer flowers have long since faded.

This plant is virtually pest-free, although it is susceptible to some slug damage in the spring. Plant it up with lots of well-rotted organic matter to condition the soil and keep it happy, then you can propagate by division in spring (never in autumn). Tall stems will need staking in windy or exposed gardens.

Iris
Iris 'Spiced Tiger'

A deeply exotic-looking version of an old favourite

Flowering time: May–June

The bearded iris is one of those classic English garden flowers whose pale blues, whites and yellows adorn planting schemes from the Edwardian borders of Gertrude Jekyll to the Eighties confections of Rosemary Verey.

All these irises have little, fuzzy beards that jut like tongues along the distinct 'falls' (these are the spreading outer petals; the higher petals are called 'standards'). Nowadays the colours have become much more exotic, which is true of this variety. *Iris* 'Spiced Tiger' was introduced only a dozen years ago and has 'broken' (or speckled) colours that range from mahogany to hot fudge sauce on vanilla ice cream. It's the horticultural equivalent of an alarmed okapi. 'Spiced Tiger' is a very individual specimen that is best grown among other, more conventional varieties.

Irises grow from knobbly roots called rhizomes; to ensure their best performance, don't plant these too deeply and position them where the shoots will get lots of sunshine. Newly planted rhizomes are vulnerable to wind rock, so when first planting, reduce the leaves by half, using a sharp knife to trim them.

Auricula
Primula auricula 'Chiquita'

An historic primula best grown in pots

Flowering time: April–May

If you hadn't seen this double auricula with your own eyes you wouldn't really think it was possible to cram this many petals into a single flower. Waves and flounces the colour of hot caramel are all squeezed together like commuters on a train. As each flower rubs shoulders with its neighbour, the general effect is of a bride's bouquet.

Auriculas were terribly popular during the nineteenth century and appeared in horticultural shows everywhere. They were so prized that they were even displayed in purpose-built auricula theatres – an arrangement of tiered staging designed to show off the glory of each flower. (There is a very fine example of an auricula theatre at Calke Abbey, in Derbyshire). However, if you don't have a theatre, they look just as good in individual pots or rock gardens.

Auriculas hate wet conditions, so plant them in sharply drained, gritty compost and protect them against the winter wet. They also thrive in full sun but need some shade from the worst of the midday heat. To increase your display, sow seed or divide plants in early spring.

Coneflower
Rudbeckia hirta 'Moreno'

A half-hardy annual that is excellent for cut flowers

Flowering time: July–October

Rudbeckias come in all sorts of shapes and sizes: from towering 2.4m (8ft) giants to small and delicate 30cm (12in) bedding varieties. *Rudbeckia hirta* 'Moreno' is one of the latter – insofar as anything quite so brazen can be delicate. Its flowers are like spinning plates of sunset-coloured petals with clear, orange-yellow tips that quiver in the wind like the tails of flustered turkeys. These surround a slightly raised, plum-coloured central boss that is crowned with a tiara of palest yellow anthers.

These rudbeckias are multi-branched and quite compact, so they make good plants for containers or the edge of borders. They are also perfect for flower arrangements as the blooms last well in water, and each plant produces plenty of them.

Plant seed on a warm windowsill between February and April, after which time you should gradually harden off the plants before planting out in May, when all risk of frost is passed.

Agastache
Agastache cana

A stunning, wildlife-friendly perennial

Flowering time: July–August

It is unlucky that this very pretty plant, native to the lower slopes of the New Mexican mountains, should be lumped with the common name of Hoary Balm of Gilead by some people. Fortunately, beneficial insects are not at all put off by this and absolutely adore this plant. The blooms attract clusters of happily buzzing bees and butterflies that settle like the lightest of kisses upon the long spikes of scented, lipstick-pink flowers.

Agastaches (the name means 'many ears' – which refers to the tubular shape of the flowers) are related to the mint family and have highly aromatic leaves and the same, squarish stems.

These plants thrive in a well-drained site in full sun. If growing from seed, sow them in situ in early spring. As a precaution, root semi-ripe cuttings in early summer in case the parent plant dies off in a particularly hard winter.

Tufted allium
Allium oreophilum

An ornamental onion suitable for light shade

Flowering time: May–June

Alliums almost invariably emerge in the shape of Father Christmas – plump and round with skinny legs. *Allium oreophilum*, however, is different: instead of the flowers being held in a ball they are much looser and surge forward like a handful of gleefully chattering shrimps tumbling out of an ivory bucket.

Each little flower of this allium (there are about fifteen to each stem) begins as a tight, dark pink bud before opening into bell-shaped, seaside-rock-coloured flowers with each petal neatly bisected by a perfect dark line. They are wonderful for injecting a bit of life into a shady corner and grow to about 20cm (8in) high.

Plant bulbs about 7.5cm (3in) deep in autumn. For more plants, gather offsets and pot them on until they are large enough to be planted outdoors. It's also easy to propagate them by collecting their little black seeds and sowing them in containers in spring.

Cyclamen
Cyclamen hederifolium

This tuberous perennial is perfect for woodlands and winter pots

Flowering time: September–October

One of the first signs of autumn is the appearance of these tiny, shuttlecock-shaped flowers that pop up just as the rest of the garden is beginning to seem a bit tired. They look as if they have been turned inside out by a high wind, and as a result they have a rather startled look – not helped by the fact that, if you look closely, the end of each flower has little pop eyes like a Mekon, straight out of the travels of Dan Dare.

These cyclamen grow particularly well around the base of trees, and their marbled leaves emerge just after the flowers. After flowering the stems twirl into neat coils in order to drop their seed.

Soak the seed overnight before sowing it in darkness as soon as it is ripe. If growing from tubers, plant them about 5cm (2in) deep with their tops at soil level. Mulch all cyclamen plants annually just as the leaves wither. Keep an eye out for marauding mice and squirrels.

Bleeding heart
Dicentra spectabilis

A clump-forming, late-spring perennial

Flowering time: May–June

The dicentra looks like a pantomime dame's washing line: a long line of freshly laundered, luminous pink joke bloomers (with white linings) blowing in the wind. Other observers have likened the plant to a Dutchman's baggy trousers (because apparently all Dutchmen dress like M C Hammer) and bleeding hearts (because of the shape of the flowers).

Either way, a dicentra is a very lively addition to an early summer border. It will happily grow to about 1m (3½ft) high and sports very becoming, mid-green leaves. If you live in a frost pocket then it would be worth giving the very soft young growth a bit of protection for the first few days. There is another, slightly more robust version that has pure white flowers.

It has thick, fleshy roots that are well suited to winter root cuttings. Seed can be sown in spring or clumps can be divided in spring or autumn.

Angel's fishing rods
Dierama pulcherrimum 'Slieve Donard hybrids'

A slim, sun-loving African perennial

Flowering time: July–August

Sometimes the common names of plants can be a little confusing, which is, after all, why the great botanist Linnaeus gave everything a smart Latin name (so that all scientists would know exactly which plant was being discussed, even if the common names in different countries were completely different.) At other times you know exactly what the name refers to. Angel's fishing rods? Of course they are.

About 1.5m (5ft) tall, and impossibly thin, the swaying stems erupt from tight clumps of grassy leaves, and from these dangle little gatherings of pink, pendant flowers that appear rather like a parade of perfectly perky chorus girls. These plants look even better if you plant them overhanging a pond where the reflection can double the pleasure.

As a member of the iris family, dierama does best when planted in full sun with a bit of shelter. If you want more plants you can grow them from seed or, preferably, from corms planted in spring. Established plants can be divided in spring.

Lenten rose
Helleborus hybridus

A classic early spring flower

Flowering time: March–April

These multi-coloured hybrid hellebores are rather like a floral version of *Joseph's Amazing Technicoloured Dreamcoat*. The Lenten rose is most often pink, but the flowers can also appear as white and yellow and taupe and mauve and claret and purple and green… (apologies to Tim Rice). This wide spectrum of colours occurs because the plants happily hybridise between each other and, as a result, new colours are always emerging. Life is sometimes one big orgy if you're a plant.

Hellebores are very delicate flowers: the petals make little Venn diagrams where they overlap and the centre is washed with minty-green. All hellebores are best seen from below as they tend to hang their heads slightly (not from modesty, but probably from embarrassment after all that hybridising). They are happy in dappled shade, and bring colour to a dull spot.

If you find a hellebore with a particularly good colour you won't be able to reproduce it from seed, but you can do so by dividing the plant after flowering in spring.

Hibiscus
Hibiscus 'Flamenco Mix'

A colourful annual that is reminiscent of the South Seas

Flowering time: July–September

In *Mutiny on the Bounty* (1962), Marlon Brando wanders around followed by gorgeous girls wearing hibiscus blooms (and not a lot else). If you wear an hibiscus flower behind your left ear it means that you are looking for love (hopefully in all the right places), whereas flaunting it on the right means that you are already taken. It's an easy way of showing who is available – much simpler than searching for wedding rings or proprietorial tattoos.

However, those flowers were cut from jungle-growing shrubs, while *Hibiscus* 'Flamenco Mix' is a much quicker and easier annual to cultivate, growing to about 1m (3½ft) high. It's almost as exotic, though, and worth wearing one Saturday night. The leaves of some varieties make an excellent boot polish when rubbed over mucky shoes.

Seed should be sown in early spring under glass before the young plant is moved to a hot spot. It is also happy and effective when planted in a container on a patio or terrace, but you should water regularly and apply a balanced liquid fertilizer every month.

Hydrangea
Hydrangea serrata 'Shojo'

A smallish shrub, perfect for border or woodland edges

Flowering time: July–September

There are shedloads of hydrangeas on sale in all sorts of different sizes, colours and shapes. *Hydrangea serrata* 'Shojo' is a lacecap hydrangea, so-called because each little four-pointed star opens consecutively so there are always little lacy gaps in the flower cover.

This variety is much more delicate than the big bath-hat-shaped flowers of the mophead varieties, and the colour is particularly delicious. The flowers begin as tiny buds the colour of glossed lips, which part to allow shell-coloured petals to emerge. These, in their turn, are edged with a deep, giggling blush of pink. The bad news is that to maintain such a downright sensuous shade you need an alkaline soil; too much acid will make it edge towards blue.

Keep plants happy by providing shelter from cold, drying winds and the worst of the midday sun. Propagate new plants from new growth, taking cuttings in spring.

Peony
Paeonia lactiflora 'Sarah Bernhardt'

A wonderful early-summer herbaceous plant

Flowering time: June–July

In this country, growing paeonies can be a bit of a gamble: the unpredictable element is the weather. If the rains come, the water will seep into all the pregnant buds and they will turn into something closely resembling wet tissues. However, if the sun smiles at flowering time, all will be glorious.

If you do succeed, you will be rewarded with one of Nature's most exquisite flowers: a great frothing confection of pink as soft and desirable as a starlet's cleavage. So, do you risk it? Oh, yes, every time. After flowering the leaves are very boring, so be sure to plant something for later in the season alongside it.

There are a few golden rules that should ensure a fine display: don't plant new specimens too deep, add lots of humus to the soil when planting, and be sure to divide congested plants in spring or sow seed for new plants in autumn. (Be patient, though, as it may take three years for the seed to germinate.)

Field poppy
Papaver rhoeas Mother of Pearl Group

A form of wild poppy that is available in many different shades

Flowering time: June–July

It is wrong to think that all field poppies are bright red. True, it is the most dominant colour, but even among the sprouting fields of Flanders after the Great War some flowers were pink or mulberry and even, like this one, stained with raspberry blotches.

The field poppy is an annual whose seeds can be dormant in the ground for many years until the earth is disturbed and growing conditions are right. Hence their appearance in cornfields (or at least those that are less troubled by selective weedkillers) after ploughing, on roadside spoil heaps and on the Somme after the shells stopped falling and the soldiers had left.

Sprinkle seed in situ in spring on soil that has been raked to a decent tilth. Thin out seedlings if they come up too close together.

Stonecrop
Sedum 'Rose Carpet'

An evergreen, spreading plant that's ideal for a border edge or rockery

Flowering time: August–September

The sedum family is one of the most diverse: there are tiny rockery sedums that look like pieces of fleshy coral, as well as big herbaceous border plants. If you have a greenhouse (or live somewhere warm) then the choice gets even larger, with varieties that hang like twisted fishnet or sprawl like overfed spiders.

Sedum 'Rose Carpet' sits somewhere in between – well-behaved, hardy everywhere and blessed by a mass of teensy little flowers that look like rosy stitches in a tapestry. The gun-metal-coloured leaves are (like all sedums) as fleshy and succulent as a Whitstable oyster – although eating them would be a mistake, as all parts of the plant are toxic.

Established plants are easily divided in springtime, or you can sow seed in containers in autumn to be planted out the following year. Sedums need full sun and good drainage to thrive.

Catchfly
Silene occulata 'Patio Mixed'

A low-growing annual that's ideal for growing in drifts or containers

Flowering time: June–October

How did this plant get the common name of catchfly? Is it a plant pollinated by flies? Does it wink seductively at passing insects? The answer is a little harsher: the stem exudes a sticky sap that works like flypaper, catching small insects. Why? Because they tried to steal nectar without pollinating the flowers, and their mistake was not being able to fly so the only way to reach the loot was by climbing the stem of the plant. But back to the story.

Catchfly is a very pretty little annual that is available in pink, red, white and blue. Dig over and rake the ground to a fine tilth before sowing seed in situ in April or May. Sow seeds in rows about 30cm (12in) apart, and thin out seedlings as they appear to one every 15cm (6in).

Cape primrose
Streptocarpus 'Caitlin'

A South African plant that's perfect for summer pots or troughs

Flowering time: all year round

This streptocarpus is not a tall plant, however, good things are said to come in small packages – look at Edith Piaf at 1.4m (4ft 8in), and Dolly Parton and St Francis of Assisi at 1.5m (5ft).

The enormous number of flowers over a long period of time is this plant's best feature. The five-petalled flowers look as if all the sorbet-pink colour has slipped into the lower half like sand through an egg timer. Streptocarpus also come in blue, purple, white and all stations in between, so there's a colour to please everyone.

As they hark from warmer climes, these plants must be brought inside for the winter if they are to survive, so grow them in pots or dig up, pot up and move them under cover before the frosts. Sow seed in late winter or take leaf cuttings in spring.

Silver lace
Tulbaghia violacea

An exquisite plant – perfect for a sheltered corner

Flowering time: May–September

Silver lace blooms with a cluster of five-pointed stars (at least 10 on each stem) that are the colour of pale candy floss, and whose centres are traced with a slightly darker raspberry cross. The stems are long and thin and supermodelly, and are covered with evergreen foliage. The lace in the name of this plant is probably a reference to a slight creamy stripe that edges the elegant, strappy leaves.

It has a remarkable vigour. When happy it will clump up well and spread itself out like a fat man on a deckchair. This plant is sometimes known as variegated society garlic (as it is a distant relative), and its leaves can be used in salads.

It's easy to grow, just sow seed in containers under glass in spring and give it full sun and good drainage. In very frosty areas plants will require a little winter protection.

Clematis
Clematis viticella 'Madame Julia Correvon'

Spectacular late-flowering climber for fences, arches and walls

Flowering time: June–September

If I had to have a wild and passionate affair with a clematis then it would have to be one of the viticella hybrids – actually, probably with more than one, so the whole thing could become rather complicated.

'Madame Julia' is very high on my list, being one of the more seductive members of the coven. It has quite large, wine-red flowers (which is no bad thing in a partner), which have slightly twisted sepals so that it sometimes seems as if it is glancing coquettishly over its shoulder with 'come-to-bed-eyes' (or maybe that is just my fevered imagination). All viticellas are late flowerers and make absolutely perfect companions for climbing roses; they start just as the roses begin to trail away.

Propagate by pinning a lightly wounded stem to the ground, where it will send out roots. After a year this new plant can be safely detached from its parent and planted elsewhere.

Meconopsis
Meconopsis punicea

A perennial with a short, but glorious, life

Flowering time: May–September

It may seem odd that something that looks as delicate as a palace made from spun sugar can withstand the inclement, and occasionally violent, weather of northern Tibet. But this little poppy is a case in point: it's a great deal tougher than it looks, so don't let those skinny, slightly hairy legs and the wide-eyed *crepe de Chine* petals fool you into providing any unnecessary luxuries.

Meconopsis punicea will grow to about 45cm (18in) high, and if it is very happy it can flower from mid-summer to early autumn. Its only quirk is that without enough water it might sulk and become monocarpic. Monocarpic plants die immediately after setting seed although, unlike annuals, they may take many years to get to that stage. Good examples are some house leeks (*Sempervivum*), saxifrages and echiums.

Meconopsis does not live that long, but preventing flowering for the first season will help it become stronger. Seed germinates easily when sown in loamless compost.

Waterlily
Nymphaea 'Rosanna Supreme'

Gorgeous floating flowers attracting darting dragonflies

Flowering time: June–September

Waterlily leaves look like the pie charts with which we all struggled in school maths lessons (although, actually, they often involved colouring, which was always a lot more fun than simultaneous equations): round and leathery but missing a perfect triangular slice. Bobbing about amongst the foliage of *Nymphaea* 'Rosanna Supreme' are the dark pink flowers that are much more complicated, with many layers of pointed petals.

The combination of circular leaves, intricate flowers and flashes of dark water are one of the most exciting things in any garden – even better if you get a glimpse of goldfish or carp swimming amongst the stems.

Ideally waterlilies should be planted in at least 20cm (8in) of water. They prefer still water, though, so don't plant them too close to fountains.

Cape daisy
Osteospermum 'Springstar Mirach'

A tender perennial infused with all the joys of life

Flowering time: July–September

These daisies are amongst the most cheerful of all plants and are always grinning. Originally they frolicked across the veldts and clustered around the kopjes of South Africa, smiling at passing impala right up to the moment that they were eaten by them. In domestic gardens they are just like a pack of very small, pink labrador puppies leaping around and enthusiastically greeting every visitor with a chorus of delight.

The Cape daisies have such simple forms and come in a wide spectrum of colours (some with different shaped petals), and provided you keep on top of the deadheading, they will happily carry on flowering until the first frosts. Even established plants need a bit of cosseting, though: lots of sun, regular water and a weekly feed.

For new plants, sow seed inside in spring or take cuttings in late summer by separating some non-flowering shoots from the base of the plants. Keep an eye out for aphids and mildew on young shoots.

Oriental poppy
Papaver orientale 'Manhattan'

A large-flowered, hardy poppy

Flowering time: June–July

All poppies are wonderful, with their slightly wrinkled, shar-pei baby petals, their depth of colour and their central bosses with their crown of black stamens that quiver like an upended beetle.

Papaver *orientale* was introduced from Turkey and, for the first couple of centuries, you could have it in any colour you liked, provided it was orange. Then breeders worked out how to get pinks and whites into the mix and wonders like this vision, 'Manhattan', in its knicker pink, became possible.

Many gardeners feel that allowing oriental poppies into your borders can be like inviting a guest on holiday only to discover that, beneath the initial charm, there lies somebody of unsound personal habits. This is because, after flowering spectacularly, these poppies tend to die very messily, so always make sure that there is something close by to take over.

Divide congested clumps of plants in spring to get more plants, or take root cuttings in autumn.

Penstemon
Penstemon 'Red Ace'

Good, strong, long-flowering plant for the summer border

Flowering time: June–September

There are a lot of penstemons available in good, strong colours, and there are also a fair few that are pretty horrible. *Penstemon* 'Red Ace' is definitely one of the good guys: perfect incarnadine trumpets hanging in long skeins upon shapely stems. If you look closely down the throat of the flower there is a small epiglottis of pearl-coloured stamens. The leaves are fairly narrow and understated, but they do hang on later than those on most deciduous plants. It should eventually reach about 40cm (16in) high and is a great plant for adding a little zip to a tired border.

Unless you want to collect seed, deadhead regularly and it will thank you by flowering for ages. Sow seed in late winter, but it is easier to propagate from cuttings in summer.

Petunia
Petunia 'Conchita Doble Velvet'

A long-flowering, trailing petunia – perfect for troughs and baskets

Flowering time: June–September

Many gardeners can get a bit sniffy about petunias because they are just regarded as easily disposable bedding plants of the sort you see in municipal window boxes and hanging baskets (busy Lizzies and trailing lobelias come into the same bracket).

It is true that petunias are not at all intellectually taxing – their name is simple to pronounce and growing them as easy as falling off a log – but they, and all bedding plants, serve their purpose very well, which is to raise a smile and lighten a leaden morning.

There are hundreds of different sorts of petunias available, in colours ranging from pure angelic white and strawberry blonde to livid, hair-raising magenta and sultry purple.

Buy petunias as young plants or sow seed under glass in full light. Pot them on and plant them outside only after the last frost. To get the best performance from petunias, give them a high-potassium feed every fortnight and never let them dry out.

Rose
Rosa 'L. D. Braithwaite'

A strong-growing rose that's perfectly sized for most gardens

Flowering time: June–October

David Austin is one of the UK's finest rose specialists, and over the past thirty years he has developed a whole new race of 'English Roses'. These have been bred from a mixture of old roses (Gallicas, Damasks, and others from the eighteenth century) and modern-day hybrid teas and floribundas.

L. D. Braithwaite was Austin's father-in-law, and he has one of the best crimson roses named in his honour. This is a clear, confident loudhailer of a rose that draws plenty attention and fulsome compliments. It has slightly tousled petals and grows to about 1m (3½ft) high and wide. It's not the most scented of roses, but you can't have everything.

Roses are susceptible to various diseases: keep an eye out for aphids (which can be sorted by ladybirds and hoverfly larvae) as well as blackspot and rust (which can be controlled by spraying early).

Tulip
Tulipa 'Maytime'

A tulip well worth tiptoeing through

Flowering time: April–May

All tulips are spectacular: their straight stems, noble bearing and gorgeous colouring announce a wonderful start to a new season, but while some tulips are like archbishops (upright, well-behaved and dressed stylishly but with decorum), others are much more outrageous.

Tulipa 'Maytime' is one of the latter: look at her, have you ever seen anything so coquettish in your life? She has a body like Jane Russell seen from behind, and with petals that look like satin and the colour of a showgirl's lipstick, she shimmies along showing off a perfectly curved (and substantial) rump with a waspish waistline.

Her presence is enough to make even the dreariest shrubs sit up, suck in their stomachs and take notice. She's a real showstopper.

Dig up the bulb after flowering and you might find little offset bulbs attached. Separate these and grow on in sandy compost until large enough for planting out.

Allium
Allium 'Firmament'

Sultry-flowered bulb for an early summer border

Flowering time: June

This is not just a rather unusual allium, but one of the very best. It is unusual because instead of being a round flower it is only about two-thirds of the sphere: an altogether more sophisticated twist on proceedings.

Allium 'Firmament' is quite new to the market and has rich, dark flowers, but with the added bonus of a slight tang of polished steel to the underside of the petals.
The closest analogy would be to a really plump, newly picked bunch of black grapes with the slight silvery bloom still intact.

The leaves of alliums are pretty rubbishy, so it's a good idea to try to hide them behind other plants. These alliums look at their best when hovering above the fresh greenness of newly emerging herbaceous plants.

Alliums are very good at seeding themselves, so if you don't cut down the dying seedheads you may get a pleasant surprise a few years down the line.

Chocolate cosmos
Cosmos astrosanguineus 'Chocamocha'

Slightly tender perennial that's perfect for containers

Flowering time: July–frost

A lot of plants are scented: in fact some gardeners might consider it the most important attribute for a garden-worthy specimen. Most flowers smell of unspecific things – some a bit fruity, some a bit peppery, some a bit like granny's bath salts, some faintly unpleasant and some spicy. Not often is there a specific, identifiable scent; however, *Cosmos astrosanguineus* 'Chocamocha' undeniably smells of chocolate.

Chocolate cosmos has a fragrance that resembles a quite sweet, milky chocolate rather than a bitter, 80 per cent cocoa-solids sort. Children, of course, are fascinated by this and so asking them to sniff this plant can be an effective diversion from such traditional pursuits as pulling the cat's tail or trying to fall into the pond. The flower is worthy of a spot in the garden, even without its scent, as it is captivatingly dark red with pretty blue-green leaves. 'Chocamocha' is a compact variety and, as such, only grows to about 30cm (12in) high.

Chocolate cosmos won't survive the winter in cold areas; the tubers should be lifted and stored in a frost-free shed until spring. As an extra insurance, plan ahead and take basal cuttings in spring.

Dahlia
Dahlia 'Aurora's Kiss'

A boldly coloured, late-flowering, tender perennial

Flowering time: July–frost

Dahlias can be admired on two levels: firstly as a long-flowering and spectacular part of any border, and secondly as the horticultural equivalent of Olympic athletes. There are well-attended dahlia shows where varieties that are totally unsuited for normal gardens are wheeled out to much oohing and aaahing – for example, the Giant Cactus varieties that have flowers 25cm (10in) wide and look like sea urchins.

Dahlia 'Aurora's Kiss' is a Miniature Ball dahlia: pretty close to spherical and with modestly sized flowers about 10cm (4in) wide. They consist of tightly grouped petals that look a little like one of those Christmas decorations that open out to form bells or Santa Claus's tummy. This variety has the deep, rich colour of carefully crushed mulberries.

In cold areas dahlia tubers should be spared the winter worst by being lifted and stored in a shed after the first frost. If you live in a borderline-cold area, or don't have anywhere suitable to store tubers, covering them with a thick mulch should be enough protection. Good drainage is vital. Propagate plants by dividing tubers in spring.

Sunflower
Helianthus annuus 'Black Magic'

Multi-branching annual that shoots above head height

Flowering time: July–October

We are used to yellow sunflowers; in fact, we are probably so used to them that they have become rather boring. France is full of fields of the things (mostly looking blackened and tired by the time we get to see them when on holiday), and children are endlessly entering competitions to grow the tallest one they can.

Helianthus *annuus* 'Black Magic' is a different matter altogether: where the yellow one is coarse (although undoubtedly cheery in demeanour), this is more suave and sophisticated. It is the same colour as a Mississippi gambler's waistcoat and every bit as louche. Even the slight shagginess of the petals makes it look as if it has been up all night losing its pearl buttons in a smoky game of five-card stud.

The seeds are large and easy to handle and should be sown in situ in spring or, if you want to grow a monster, inside in late winter.

Iris
Iris 'Ecstatic Night'

Gorgeously coloured bearded iris

Flowering time: May–June

This might seem a little weird but there are some plants that look as if they would make the most divine underwear. This iris is a case in point.

The colour of *Iris* 'Ecstatic Night' is the most decadent that Nature has ever invented; it is the colour of the curtains in a Circassian bordello, of mulberry juice trickling down the chin of a Maharajah and of black cherry jam spread on fresh granary bread. The petals look like the most perfect Florentine velvet and feel smooth and warm to the touch. They look wonderful in a border, and especially as an edging to a path.

All irises are hardy in the UK. They are best planted in late summer or early autumn in well-drained soil. Lift and divide clumps if they get too large, which should improve the flowering.

Pincushion flower
Scabiosa atropurpurea 'Chile Black'

A half-hardy perennial that adds a sultry fruitiness to late summer

Flowering time: July–September

Many really good flowers, like particularly plump and smiling babies, look good enough to eat. This is one of them, with its little bite-sized buttons that are made up of an aureole of petals that are the colour of blackcurrants steeped in vintage port and which are peppered with white anthers that look like fine shavings of freshly picked coconut. (The anthers being the pollen-bearing part of the stamens – the male part – in a flower.)

Scabiosa atropurpurea 'Chile Black' looks spectacular when set against the deep oranges and yellows of late summer. And the taste? I would hope that it would taste slightly chocolatey with a firm alcoholic undertow but, sadly, it would probably taste of dust, so it's best to leave the whole notion safely in the imagination.

Scabious hate wet conditions and may perish in a cold winter. Collect seed in autumn as a precaution and sow it in spring if you lose plants. Take basal cuttings in spring.

Tulip
Tulipa 'Black Parrot'

Luxuriant, deep-purple tulip that's perfect in pots

Flowering time: May

The parrot tulips are the most over-the-top of all tulips. While most of their species maintain an aloof dignity, these throw caution to the wind and appear in public with mad, deranged grins and flyaway petals. They are like Barbara Cartland emerging from a spin dryer: frilly petals akimbo, fringes waving, tassels twirling and streaks of colour racing through every pore. That said, *Tulipa* 'Black Parrot' is extraordinarily conservative in comparison.

Sadly, there are others that do not exercise the same admirable restraint: one called 'Estella Rijnveld' looks like a tornado in a raspberry ripple factory, 'Gemma' is like an overweight welder in a tutu, and 'Professor Rontgen' really should know better.

Tulip bulbs should be planted in November, later than daffodils and many others. They perform best in well-drained soil and should be planted about 15cm (6in) deep. Ideally, all bulbs should be lifted after flowering and ripened in a greenhouse, ready for the next season.

Columbine
Aquilegia vulgaris 'Adelaide Addison'

A great perennial for the border or a gravel garden

Flowering time: May

There is a great swarming host of aquilegia hybrids, of which *Aquilegia vulgaris* 'Adelaide Addison' is a fine example. Native to North America, this variety reaches about 60cm (2ft) high and has ferny foliage.

Long spurs like kite tails stream from the back of the flowers, and contain nectar held in just the right place for long-tongued pollinators. The petals of this particular double-flowered variety are just like the skirts of a dancer in a Wild West saloon (the ones doing a high-kicking dance while wearing button-up boots and long flouncey knickers before running screaming into the wings just as an enormous fight begins). Aquilegia self-seed readily and are always producing new shapes and colours.

These plants are easy to grow from seed, but if you want an exact replica of the parent then you should grow them in complete isolation to any other aquilegias. Sow seed when ripe or save until spring.

Clematis
Clematis 'Ashva'

A subtly coloured, large-flowered cultivar

Flowering time: June–September

The A-level chemists among you will know the word chromatography; the rest of us will scratch our heads until we faintly remember lessons spent dropping drips of chemicals onto blotting paper and observing how the colours spread. The flowers of *Clematis* 'Ashva' show the same effect: a rich purple, with a centre of plum that starts quite intensely, but then leaches away like brandy spilt on sand to leave only the faintest memory of its presence.

This is not the tallest clematis available, only reaching about 1.5–2m (5–6½ft), so it is best grown on a frame rather than trying to get it to cover a wall or trellis.

This is a Group 3 clematis, which means it produces stems and flowers in the season after it has been pruned, so it should be cut back to a pair of strong buds 30cm (12in) above the ground in about February.

Virgin's bower
Clematis x *durandii*

A short-growing, but long-flowering climber

Flowering time: July–August

Where would we be without clematis? They come in almost every colour and size, and there are representatives of this family that will keep the garden in flower through most months of the year.

Clematis x *durandii* is an herbaceous clematis that has dusty purple, four-pointed flowers that look like one of those windmills children use to decorate sandcastles. It only reaches about 1.2m (4ft) high, so it is not the one to choose if you are after a florally clad arch or trellis. It is, however, charming in a mixed border, where it can scramble over a pyramid or drape itself over a shrub. Many spring-flowering bushes look a bit dreary later in the season, but a clematis scrambling through their branches has the same effect as putting fairy lights on a Christmas tree.

Prune to about 20cm (8in) in early spring. Propagate plants by rooting softwood cuttings in spring or summer, or layer it by pinning a shoot to the ground in autumn.

Snow crocus
Crocus sieberi

An early-flowering bulb, perfect for cheering up winter

Flowering time: February–March

Imagine this: you wake up on a cold morning, fling back the curtains and the world is white. You rush outside and there, poking through the snow, are the javelin heads of crocus.

Crocus sieberi has closed petals that are veined as delicately as a mouse's ear. As the day warms it begins to open, shaking off the clinging flakes of snow, to reveal a deep purple throat with an egg-yellow centre that gapes like a hungry fledgling. A wonderful sight when all around is cold and the colours of spring seem a long way away. This crocus is perfect for naturalising in large drifts, or for close planting in a shallow bowl or pot.

Plant bulbs 9mm (⅜in) deep in autumn, preferably in gritty soil that will replicate its natural mountainside habitat. Crocus needs a sunny spot to make the flowers open properly.

Morning glory
Ipomoea tricolor 'Grandpa Otts'

A fast growing, annual climber

Flowering time: August–October

A perfect plant for quickly covering a trellis or fence, morning glory has strong tendrils that stretch and wind like a box of snakes. This climber carries lots of mid-green leaves that are shaped like hearts, and its trumpet-shaped flowers are dark purple with a glowing red star around a clear white epicentre. From August until the first frosts this plant will produce hundreds of blooms that slowly emerge as the sun rises, only to have faded to husks by lunchtime.

One of this plant's close relations is the insidious bindweed, a perfect example of how short a step it is between glory and the incinerator. As Grandpa Otts was, apparently, a Baptist minister from Iowa, he'd have appreciated his namesake's redemptive qualities.

Start under glass early in spring; chip seeds with a knife and soak for 24 hours before sowing. The plant is very popular with bees.

Sweet pea
Lathyrus odoratus 'Katie Alice'

A sky-blue annual climber, perfect for cut flowers

Flowering time: late spring–early summer

The sweet pea has about the best scent of anything anywhere – not just better than most other flowers, but better than newly mown grass, baking bread, brewing coffee, the heads of small babies, the biscuity paws of puppies or the scented wrists of courtesans. The bounty does not stop there, however, as sweet peas are also unbelievably generous with their flowers. A few plants growing up a pyramid will give you countless vases of sweet-smelling blooms all summer. The main problem that then arises is finding enough places for all the flowers; you must keep picking because if you do not the plant will start setting seed and the flowering will slow right down. There are colours available that will suit every taste.

As it is an annual climber, seed should be sown under glass in autumn or spring. Seed must be soaked or chipped prior to sowing to aid germination. The plant is happy grown on wigwams of poles or on a trellis.

Pasque flower
Pulsatilla vulgaris

Very beautiful native plant that thrives in rockeries

Flowering time: April

Some of you may remember the twin sons of Isaac: Jacob was a smooth man and Esau was a hairy man (there was a argument over a 'mess of pottage'). This plant is an Esau: stem, leaves and some of the actual flower are covered in very fine hairs.

The heavy-headed blooms vary in colour from white to flushed purple and are quite large, about 7cm (3in) across. They usually flower around Easter (hence the name Pasque flower). The hairy theme then continues as the very lovely seedheads are even fuzzier.

Pulsatilla is native in the wild in this country, but it is becoming increasingly rare as the chalk grassland in which it thrives is disappearing. Do not eat the plant, as it will cause a nasty stomach upset.

Needs extremely sharp drainage as winter wet can easily kill it. Plant when small, as it hates its roots being disturbed later. Sow seed in summer as soon as it is ripe.

Annual sage
Salvia horminum 'Blue Denim'

A late-flowering annual for bedding and containers

Flowering time: July–September

Some of you may remember a cheesy advertisement from the Seventies for an aftershave called Denim (much beloved by unwashed teenagers. I know, I was one of them). The tagline was 'Denim... for men who don't have to try too hard', which was illustrated with a picture of a finely manicured female hand fondling its way across a very hairy chest.

This is just a simple, annual sage: the blue is extraordinarily intense and irresistible, with flushes of blackcurrant around the edges – difficult for any hand to resist picking. The leaves and stems are also almost as hairy as a Seventies rug.

The colour comes not from the flowers but from the bracts (modified leaves that surround a rather insignificant flower). Sow seed in well-prepared ground in spring.

African blue lily
Agapanthus africanus 'Blue Globe'

A South African native that provides spectacular colour in late summer

Flowering time: August–September

It is odd in gardening how one man's meat is another man's poison: things that some people consider weeds are rare and lovely garden plants to others. Arum lilies (*Zantedeschia aethiopica*) are hunted down in New Zealand, and in South Africa agapanthus grows on roadside verges in the same way that thistles do on the central reservations of European motorways. Except the agapanthus is prettier. It seems weird that the agapanthus we much admire is treated with the same disdain there as we hold for dandelions.

Agapanthus *africanus* 'Blue Globe' is undoubtedly spectacular, with great bunches of pure blue flowers held like lamplighter's torches on long, elegant stems. The plants look particularly effective in large terracotta pots, especially as they flower much better if kept slightly pot-bound and constricted.

These plants hate waterlogged or heavy soil but still need plenty of moisture, and will suffer if allowed to dry out completely. Propagate by dividing well-established clumps in mid-spring.

Aster
Aster 'Little Carlow'

A charming and elegant daisy for late summer and early autumn

Flowering time: August–October

Asters (or Michaelmas daisies) are often perceived as quite granny-ish plants. They flower vigorously but can be a bit leprous being almost always stricken with the white bloom of mildew.

'Little Carlow' is slightly different: for a start it is not one of the novi-belgii cultivars, but a hybrid of the much tougher *A. cordifolius*. The flower is much more *soignée*: instead of closely bunched and, frankly, rather lumpy blooms we have clouds of daisies the colour of thrice-washed denim. The centres are a refreshing yellow, and the leaves are small and heart-shaped.

Best in moderately fertile, moist soil in semi-shade, but it will tolerate full sun at a push. Divide plants in spring, replanting only the most vigorous shoots. Seed can be sown spring or autumn.

Delphinium
Delphinium elatum 'Joan Edwards'

A perennially popular plant, known by all and loved by most

Flowering time: spring–summer

'**There** once was a Dormouse who lived in a bed, Of delphiniums (blue) and geraniums (red).' All was well until some interfering doctor came along and changed all his flowers to yellow and white chrysanthemums, after which the dormouse seldom opens his eyes again. It is all in the A.A. Milne poem if you want to know more, but my instincts say that, given the choice, most people would opt for delphiniums over yellow chrysanthemums.

Delphinium *elatum* 'Joan Edwards' is one of the everlasting classics of the herbaceous border. Soaring spires of gorgeous blue add enormous solidity and spectacle to mid-summer borders. This is a plant that was born to dance with old-fashioned roses, creamy lupins and red geraniums.

Best in full sun out of strong winds, it needs staking in about March before it starts growing. Propagate from basal cuttings (the thickness of a pencil) taken in early spring. Watch out for slugs.

Liverwort
Hepatica nobilis

A winter flower for the woodland

Flowering time: February–May

It sometimes seems that, every so often, when taxonomists are getting bored of sitting there naming plants all day, they liven things up by dumping an appalling name on some poor, unfortunate plant. Thus this spectacular (though tiny) plant is lumped with the common name of liverwort because it was used as a medicinal herb and the three-lobed leaves resemble the human liver.

The flowers are clear purple-blue and, if you are very lucky, are even better when pushing through the lightest covering of snow. The magenta-splashed leaves appear a few days after the flowers. Hepaticas are found all over the world from Japan to Scandinavia via the Carpathian Mountains.

Best in a shady garden. Sow seed in summer or you can divide plants, but they will be slow to recover. There is a danger of slug damage when plants are young.

Beardless iris
Iris 'Broadleigh Penny'

An elegant flower for lightly-shaded places

Flowering time: May–June

This is a hybrid taken from the irises of the Pacific Coast and is without the characteristic fluffy goatee beards that the more popular German irises have. They are, however, no less lovely, and in fact they can be more useful in mixed plantings as they will tolerate a bit of overshadowing by other plants, so they are ideal for areas of light shade under shrubs.

Where *Iris germanica* has large flowers with ostentatious frills, this hybrid is more like a sleek Californian surfer with slim leaves and cinch-waisted petals. The flowers are occasionally mistaken for orchids because of the subtle colours and prominent markings on each petal.

Seeds should be chilled after sowing by placing them, and their container, in a fridge (not a freezer) for three weeks. Irises prefer neutral to acid soil. Divide in autumn.

Himalayan blue poppy

Meconopsis 'Willie Duncan'

A serene and breathtakingly gorgeous perennial poppy

Flowering time: April

This is possibly one of the bluest flowers in the world. *Meconopsis* 'Willie Duncan' is the blue of Everest skies, of glacial torrents over glass smooth pebbles and of the sparkling eyes of Nordic princesses. To see them in a drift under the young lime-coloured leaves of immature trees is a near-spiritual experience.

The seed of this poppy variety was first brought to the UK in 1924 by the famous plant hunter Frank Kingdon Ward, to immediate sensation. A poppy this colour was a revelation and, by 1927, there were huge public displays in London and Edinburgh.

The Himalayan blue poppy is a plant that needs acid soil and it grows particularly well in the cooler, rainier parts of the country (particularly Scotland and the south west).

Sow seed thinly in pots as soon as it is ripe (late spring) in loamless seed compost. Mulch adult plants generously with leaf mould. Grows to about 1.2m (4ft) high.

Love-in-a-mist
Nigella hispanica 'Midnight'

A heavenly annual that is ridiculously easy to grow

Flowering time: June–August

If there's a top ten of the easiest plants to grow then this is in the top five. Instructions for use are as follows: sprinkle a packet of seed around in spring and then go off and have a drink. That's all. Within a short space of time you will be rewarded by a sea of lazy-eyed, dusky blue flowers surrounded by a fine froth of feathery foliage.

The flowers of nigella are the love, the leaves are the mist and the combination is captivating. It doesn't stop there, though: as the blooms fade they morph into puffy, spider-legged seedpods. As the autumn approaches, these pods split and shiny black seeds are spread around the garden.

It is a supremely romantic plant where both flowers and seedpods are perfect for picking and flower arranging. This plant also comes in paler blue, white and degrees of pink. Totally trouble-free.

Sand phlox
Phlox bifida 'Ralph Haywood'

A low-growing plant with lots of scented flowers; good in rockeries

Flowering time: late April

There are a lot of different phloxes around and all of them are native to North America – except one lonely Siberian. They range from tall ones in many colours, which are best for the late summer border, to small annuals that are suitable for bedding out.

Phlox bifida 'Ralph Haywood' is a scampering little perennial that forms neat evergreen mounds which grow to about 20cm (8in) high. The official botanical description of the flowers is that they are 'salverform and borne in abundant cymes'. Roughly translated this means that there are lots of flat-topped, pleasantly fragrant, star-shaped flowers that look a little like paper doilies – albeit rather superior ones. They are a rather comforting deep lavender blue, like the bath salts sold at village fêtes.

Propagate from softwood cuttings taken from non-flowering stems in spring. The plants are happy in poor, well-drained soil and will thrive in either full sun or slightly dappled shade.

Sage
Salvia patens 'Dot's Delight'

Palest blue tender plant for pots or borders

Flowering time: July–October

Behold one of the finest members of the large sage family: a genus with about nine hundred assorted aunts, uncles and cousins from all over the world. This is a tender Mexican perennial that is perfect for filling post-bulb gaps and adding a little class to late-summer borders (when things tend to get a little straggly and rowdy).

The flower is shaped like the wide-open beak of an exotic bird swooping down to snatch an unsuspecting mouse from the bosom of its family. Except that, in spite of the cavernous maw, this plant is far too delicate to be carnivorous; if it was a bird of prey it would probably only eat windfall apples and fairy cakes.

Sow seed in mid-spring or take basal cuttings in late summer. Protect young seedlings from the rapacious ways of slugs and snails. Needs plenty of sunshine and good drainage.

Horned violet
Viola 'Columbine'

Short and delicately coloured violet that flowers all summer

Flowering time: May–August

One of the popular activities amongst pre-school children is marbling paper. This involves floating colourful dollops of paint on water and then dipping paper into the mixture. These are then brought back home so that proud parents can stick them on the fridge. This little violet looks as if it has been put through this process.

A pale, cream-coloured flower, *Viola* 'Columbine' appears to have been dragged through a sky blue puddle that has resulted in remarkably pretty veining across its tiny petals. It is only about 20cm (8in) high and makes a really excellent, long-flowering, front-of-border plant. The leaves are heart-shaped and the flowers make an exciting addition to a salad – more for the colour than the taste.

Cut back after the first flush of flowers and it will happily repeat all summer. Sow seed when ripe or save until spring. Save seed in paper envelopes in a dry place.

Clematis
Clematis florida 'Alba Plena'

Extravagantly flowered, mid-sized climber

Flowering time: June–September

The clematis family has an enormous range of colours and shapes. Some have simple four-point, star-like flowers, some elegant, hanging bells and others have vast flowers the size of one of the Queen Mother's hats. All are the result of many, many years of tweaking and fiddling by plant breeders.

Clematis florida 'Alba Plena' is one of the larger flowered varieties – with knobs on. With a central tiara of petals the colour of lime juice, it looks like a mutant waterlily. It blooms in mid-summer and, as the flowers age, the green fades from the petals and they turn pure angelic white before they die. There is another double version with a deep purple centre. Grows to about 3m (10ft) high. Clematis like their roots to be cool, so it is important to provide some shade at the base of the plant. Prune hard in early spring.

Spurge
Euphorbia 'Redwing'

Useful evergreen for a sunny, well-drained site

Flowering time: March–April

This picture is of a plant on the brink.
It was taken in March, early in the morning.
In a couple of weeks that bud will open to
reveal bracts the colour of greenfinch
breasts on reddish stems. (A bract is not
strictly speaking a flower, but a sort of
modified leaf: however, in many spurges it
is often the most striking part of the plant.
There is a flower behind it, but it is tiny.)

Euphorbia 'Redwing' is evergreen and
modest in its habits, making a clump about
60cm (2ft) across.

Cut back old flower stems after flowering,
but beware of the milky sap that oozes
from the plant when cut – it can burn
those with sensitive skins.

Galtonia
Galtonia viridiflora

A serene spire for late summer

Flowering time: August–September

It is tempting to think that only spring flowers (like daffodils, bluebells and tulips) are grown from bulbs. Although that is mostly correct, there are some real corkers that flower later from bulbs, and this is one of them. Galtonias have deep emerald, strap-shaped leaves and send up 75cm (2½ft) tall flower spikes, from which swing a couple of dozen waxy bells streaked with pale green that are wonderful in flower arrangements. The whole thing is very like a multi-storey, out-of-season snowdrop that exerts a calming influence on some of the brighter coloured, late-flowering plants. If you were a wandering elf caught out in the rain, the flowers would also make perfect hats.

Plant bulbs deeply in spring but do not allow them to get waterlogged. Propagate from offset bulbs or from seed sown in trays during autumn. Protect bulbs with a winter mulch in frosty areas.

Sunflower
Helianthus annuus 'Jade'

Unusual, pale sunflower that works well in herbaceous borders

Flowering time: July–September

I bet you thought that there was nothing simpler than a sunflower. Wrong. For example, did you realise that what we think is the flower is not? Instead it is called the head and it is made up of hundreds of tiny flowers (called disc florets); the halo of petals are actually ray florets. If you look closely you can see that the florets are arranged in perfect mathematical spirals.

While in bud, sunflowers also demonstrate heliotropism: they move in order to keep the sun in their faces, rather like an obsessive sunbather moving a lounger around the pool. However, as soon as the flowers emerge they stop moving – usually when facing east. *Helianthus annuus* 'Jade' is a very pretty variety, sporting attractive green-tinted petals.

The seed can be dried for birdfood or roasted as a snack or to add a bit of crunch to salads. It can also be processed into biodiesel.

Corsican hellebore
Helleborus argutifolius

An invaluable, winter-flowering, evergreen perennial

Flowering time: March

Some might consider this a rather dull plant; with heavy green leaves and pale green flowers, it's not exactly a carnival with marching bands and high-stepping baton twirlers. But sometimes subtle is good, especially when there are hidden delights.

The pleasure of *Helleborus argutifolius* is mostly in the detail. Look closely at the leaves: their edges are finely cut like the teeth of a shark and marbled with fine white veins. The flowers are a great teeming mass of palest green, the colour of pistachio ice cream, but on even closer inspection there is a yellow spider of stamens sheltering in the centre of each bonnet-shaped flower. No matter how cold the weather, you should always take the time to look.

Happy in both sun and partial shade. Best propagated from seed sown fresh in spring; it is unsuitable for division as it only grows on a single stem.

Golden hop
Humulus lupulus 'Aureus'

A vigorous, herbaceous climber

Flowering time: September

Some climbers are sedate and well behaved. Roses, for example, can easily be trained to cover a wall or drape themselves insouciantly across a gateway; the clematis is a little wilder, but still malleable; then, at the other end of the scale, there is the Russian vine (*Fallopia baldschuanica*) – a plant that is capable of colonising small countries or smothering outlying villages if given the chance.

Somewhere in the middle is the hop: a fast-growing, herbaceous (meaning that it dies back to nothing in winter) climber that can shin up a 5m (16½ft) tree or along a fence in the space of a season. It is grown for its bright, greenish-yellow leaves and clusters of wafery flowers that hang like chandeliers in late summer.

This plant tends to sucker a bit, so be careful when deciding where to plant it; the plus side is that new plants are easy to make by digging up runners.

Torch flower
Kniphofia 'Ice Queen'

A sturdy, upright, late summer perennial

Flowering time: July–September

To many people the kniphofia family means one thing: red hot pokers. These plants have rather disreputable-looking red tips and pale yellow tails thrusting from tangles of spiky leaves: the sort of plant you either love or despise. So what do you call one that is neither red nor hot?

In the case of *Kniphofia* 'Ice Queen' you could call it a Chic Poker. It may not roll off the tongue as easily, but instead of glowing harlot-scarlet flowers there are modish pokers wearing tasteful frocks of greenish-yellow, and the unsophisticated foliage is swapped for neater, spined leaves. It is a poker more likely to be found taking tea in musical salons than loafing around with disreputable sharks in basement billiard halls.

This plant is easily grown from seed, although its progeny is never exactly like the parents. Divide established clumps in late spring. Be warned that they provide good hiding places for snails.

French lavender
Lavandula stoechas 'Tiara'

A heavily scented, grey-leaved lavender that's great in pots

Flowering time: May–August

Everybody knows about lavender: dark purple-blue, strongly scented and often found in little bags at the back of grandmother's chest of drawers. *Lavandula stoechas* 'Tiara' is a slightly less hardy relation. The most obvious difference is the coxcomb of cream-green petals that stick vertically upwards (it is sometimes referred to as 'Bunny Ears' lavender). Below these protuberances is a chubby, tubular body that is studded with tiny, jewel-like, blue inflorescences that makes it look like a strange, mythical insect. It is a little shorter than other lavenders but should manage to flower twice if you cut it back after the first flush in late May.

Needs shelter from bitter winds and good winter drainage. Propagate from semi-ripe cuttings in summer or from seed sown under glass in spring. Hang in an airing cupboard to dry the flowers.

Agapanthus
Agapanthus 'Mercury'

An easily grown and very chic perennial

Flowering time: August–September

In 1952 Cyd Charisse (you will have seen her twirling all over the shop with Gene Kelly in *Singing in the Rain* – and if you haven't, you should be ashamed of yourself) took out a $5 million insurance policy on her legs. They were so extraordinarily long and shapely that the nearest thing we have to them today is the stem of an agapanthus flower (albeit without knees). Elegant and smooth, they arch away from the tightly bunched leaves carrying their precious burden of petals. In the case of *Agapanthus* 'Mercury' it is a spilling over of pure white bells that open in swift succession like a flurry of startled penguins leaping from a cliff. The anthers within each flower are darker and contrasting.

Sow seed (with some heat) in autumn or spring, but bear in mind that it will be at least two years before it flowers. Most seedlings will not exactly match the parent.

Kazakh allium
Allium karataviense

A very decorative, short allium whose flowers are well suited for drying

Flowering time: April

All alliums are, at heart, just posh onions. There are lots of them in all sorts of sizes and colours, ranging from imperial purple to clear Caribbean blue. They are mostly native to the northern hemisphere, from America all the way to China. *Allium karataviense* comes from the Black Mountains (Kara Tau) in Kazakhstan where it grows on well-drained scree that is bitterly cold in winter and hot in summer.

The Kazakh allium has a relatively short stem (presumably to prevent it being blown across a steppe by a fierce gust of wind) and wonderful bluish-grey leaves that look like dolphin's flippers.
The clustering florets are white and held on individual stalks, so that the whole thing looks like a big dandelion clock.

Plant bulbs in autumn about 7.5cm (3in) deep, preferably in a sunny spot. Propagate from seed sown in spring, although it will happily self-seed if it wants.

Mountain knapweed
Centaurea montana 'Alba'

Mat-forming, woolly-stemmed perennial

Flowering time: May–July

Centaurea montana is one of those plants that some consider a delight, some dismiss as a roadside flower and others damn as an interfering weed. Yes, it does poke its nose from the sunny side of central reservations and hedgerows (a pleasure to drive past) and, yes, it will breed without blushes all over a dryish border and may possibly become a minor irritation (could be worse, could be ground elder or rabbits). But the indisputable fact remains that it has a remarkably striking flower. Beginning in a tight, scaly, hand-grenade-shaped bud it sprouts sparkly petals that look like a cross between a piece of complicated origami and a delicate cogwheel around a darkly speckled centre.

Sow seed in late summer or start root cuttings in winter. Will tolerate a little shade provided the ground is not too dry. It reaches a height of about 45cm (18in).

Cosmos
Cosmos bipinnatus 'Psyche White'

An elegant, self-supporting annual

Flowering time: June–October

If plants had roles, *Cosmos bipinnatus* 'Psyche White' would be a prima ballerina. Perfect and lissom with pure, virginal white, semi-double, tissue-paper flowers pirouetting and glissading in the wind atop slender legs barely covered by wispy shreds of leaf.

Provided the seed is sown early enough this flower will emerge in about June, starting small but swiftly rising to a Grand Pas. Then, after the corps de ballet of the border have completed their mid-summer performance and have fallen to the ground, she will carry on until the final frosted curtain of winter forces her from the stage. She is perfect for filling any mid-border gaps, and has equally fetching sisters who come in shades of pink.

Sow under cover (with some heat) in early spring, harden off in a cold frame and plant out after the last frosts. Grow in full sun. Also try *Cosmos bipinnatus* 'Purity'.

Lenten rose
Helleborus hybridus

A popular and easily grown plant for shade

Flowering time: March–April

The more observant among you will have noticed that this particular hellebore has already featured in this book: different colour, but essentially the same plant. It appears in two different places because of its position as Master of Confusion. A pink parent can produce offspring that are anything from dusky purple to clear pearly white, like this one. The flowers can also be both single and double but all have a very attractive, five-part seed pod that looks like a cluster of snuggly mussels clinging to a rock.

Helleborus *hybridus* is about the easiest variety of hellebore to grow, and pretty well looks after itself. It is generally happy in almost any soil except waterlogged and excessively dry conditions.

Hellebores are sometimes susceptible to aphid infestations and leaf spot; old and infected leaves should be cut off and burnt as the disease will sometimes survive in the compost heap. All parts of the plant are poisonous.

Tree hydrangea
Hydrangea paniculata 'Everest'

Elegant, large shrub, fine in sun or light shade, that flowers in late summer

Flowering time: August–September

Not for this hydrangea the flat crew cut or mopheaded (always an unfortunate and rather unflattering metaphor) flowers of its more common brothers. Not for it the tiresome changing of colour from blue to pink depending on the alkalinity of the soil. *Hydrangea paniculata* 'Everest' will always have her creamy-white flowers and elegantly pointed panicles that fade to very pale pink in the sunshine.

The shrub itself is pretty fast growing and will get to about 5m (16½ft) tall with a spread of 3m (10ft). It looks fabulous as a spectacular feature plant at the back of a large mixed border or on the lighter margins of a woodland garden. Cut it back quite hard in spring, though, if you want larger flowerheads.

This plant is sterile and will not set seed so it is best propagated from cuttings. Either take softwood (new growth) cuttings in spring or hardwood (old growth) in winter. Flowers may be removed and dried.

Iris
Iris 'Elizabeth Poldark'

An impeccably tasteful iris: white and haughty, with frills

Flowering time: mid-May–late June

This iris has magnificently ruffled flowers of purest white with just the slightest sniggle of yellow at the base of the petals and on the tips of its downy beard. Can you imagine this iris standing alone but magnificent on a cliff: hair flaring in the teeth of a brisk sou'wester as she frets over a smuggler's pitching barque? Maybe this is getting a little too far-fetched but these flowers do have a wonderfully dramatic shape only enhanced by their glowing colour. Please do not take the imagery literally – irises should never be planted on top of cliffs and nowhere near salt spray!

For the best performance, it needs to be in a very sunny border and should not be shaded by other plants. Avoid fertilisers and covering the rhizomes with mulch.

Regal lily
Lilium regale

A tall, heavily scented, bulbous perennial that's invaluable in any garden

Flowering time: July–August

Not only is this about the easiest lily to grow, it is also the most wondrous. The stems are tall, willowy and supremely elegant. The flowers are like the trumpets of the angelic host – pure white with pale pink flushes. They have long been a symbol of both peace and purity (often seen in paintings of the Virgin Mary from the fourteenth century Siennese masters right up to the pre-Raphaelites).

The scent of regal lilies is nothing short of heavenly: sometimes so sweet as to be almost overpowering. It is strongest in the evening – as is often the case with white-flowered plants because they are trying to attract pollinating moths. The yellow pollen can stain clothes, so try not to get too close or cut them out if you bring flowers indoors for arrangements.

Plant bulbs at least 12cm (5in) deep in well-drained, light soil in autumn. Watch out for bright red lily beetles (and their repulsive, filth-covered offspring) in spring and summer, squashing them before they chew through all the leaves.

Tobacco plant
Nicotiana sylvestris

An imposing annual with a head of cascading flowers

Flowering time: August–September

The scene is set: a late summer evening, a comfortable deckchair, a glass of something cold and a satisfying glow after a day of productive gardening. As the last warmth of its rays ebbs away, the sun finally slips below the horizon and one by one the stars begin to twinkle. This is the hour of the nicotiana.

The first thing you will notice is the scent: sweeter than syrup, spicier than saffron and headier than jasmine; the second is the luminosity of the white flowers – as dusk falls each sticky blossom, head hung in supplication, seems to glow.
During the day this plant is pretty, but come the night it's transformed into an irresistible enchantress.

Nicotiana is an annual easily grown from seed that reaches about 1.2m (4ft) high. Sow in spring and prick out into 8cm (3½in) pots before planting out into the border when all risk of frost is past. Will thrive in part-shade or sun.

Moroccan daisy
Rhodanthemum 'African Eyes'

Perky evergreen daisy suitable for most parts of the garden

Flowering time: spring–late summer

If you were of a paranoid turn of mind then the sheer abundance of these eyes following your every move might make you feel a little queasy. *Rhodanthemum* 'African Eyes' is a low-growing evergreen perennial with filigree, silvery leaves. But its best feature is a teeming mass of creamy-white, dark-pupilled daisies that stand and stare like a horde of starving orphans eyeing up a roast chicken.

These plants are very well behaved and look great in rockeries (they are native to the stonier parts of North Africa), containers, gravel gardens or border edgings. They flower without ceasing from spring until late summer and all it wants from you is sun, good drainage and, of course, constant admiration.

Easily grown from seed sown in a cold frame in spring or from softwood cuttings in June. It will cope with any soil, provided it is not waterlogged, and is hardy almost anywhere in Britain.

Rose

Rosa 'Flower Carpet White' (syn. 'Noaschnee')

Short, long-flowering rose suitable for containers

Flowering time: spring–autumn

It is difficult to imagine gardens without white roses; few plants are as iconic. Where would the white garden at Sissinghurst be without roses? Weddings without white roses would also be lacking a certain something. Yorkshire would not be the same with a marigold as an emblem, and chocolate-box cottages would be less irresistible without white roses arching over their doors.

Rosa 'Flower Carpet White' has double, pure white flowers (with a slight ivory blush to the base of the petals). This rose reaches about 60cm (2ft) high. Pruning is important to prevent it becoming straggly and losing shape: cut just above an outward-facing bud in autumn or spring.

Foam flower
Tiarella cordifolia 'Iron Butterfly'

A great, long-flowering plant for deep or semi-shade

Flowering time: May

I don't know whether any of you have ever been to Ibiza; not the countryside, the wildflowers and the native fauna (although they have a great deal to offer), but the nightclubbing end of things. If so, you may have attended a foam party where the entire dancefloor is swamped with froth – I imagine the experience is similar to wading around inside a pint of Guinness. Anyway, that is how a ladybird must feel if it got caught up in this plant. A mass of gorgeous, white, starry flowers with tiny, peach-coloured stamens swarming along multiple stems. The heart-shaped leaves turn bronze-red in autumn. Sadly, it would never survive on Ibiza, as it needs some shade.

Protect from excessive winter wet by ensuring that there is enough drainage in the soil. Excellent as ground cover in woodland gardens. Sow seed or divide in spring. It spreads easily.

Silky wisteria
Wisteria brachybotrys 'Shiro-kapitan'

A classic large climber for covering walls, trees, fences and pergolas

Flowering time: June

There are few things more magnificent than an ancient, knobbly-trunked wisteria twining its way around ancient stone pillars and across the sturdy timbers of an old pergola (there is a particularly good one at Eltham Palace, south London).

Wisteria *brachybotrys* 'Shiro-kapitan' has magnificent racemes of flowers that drip like pearl earrings from amongst soft green leaves. The bases of the scrubbed-white flowers are washed with a clear yellow stain. These are followed by velvety, bean-like seed pods that are about 20cm (8in) long. There are many other wisteria varieties available, most of which have violet-blue flowers. Pruning is very important if you want optimum flowering – as a general rule prune to five buds in August and three in February.

The stems of wisteria twine anti-clockwise around any support, which is useful to know if you are tying it in. Propagate from sideshoot basal cuttings in summer or by layering in autumn. This variety will reach a height of about 10m (33ft).

Golden garlic
Allium moly 'Jeannine'

A perfect allium for the wilder parts of the garden

Flowering time: June

Most alliums have round pom-pom flowers in shades of mauve, claret and purple, so when confronted with a flower the colour of a new-born chick, an allium is not the first thing that springs to mind. Smell it and all those misgivings drift away. Every part of all alliums smell of onion – the leaves, the stems, the flowers and the bulbs (which is a convincing reason as to why they are not good in flower arrangements – unless they have been dried, in which case they are marvellous and very long-lasting). This particular variety, 'Jeannine', is about 30cm (12in) high with much bigger flowers than the species parent. Each plant has about thirty star-shaped yellow flowers hanging from each umbel (or stem).

'Jeannine' spreads quickly, so it's perfect for naturalising in light woodland or the shrub border. Plant bulbs in autumn or sow seed in containers in spring.

African daisy
Arctotis adpressa 'Hayley'

The African daisy is a cheerful addition to summer pots

Flowering time: June–October

Some of you might remember that great 1980s' invention, the Ra-Ra skirt. This was a very short, flared skirt usually worn with suede ankle boots and opaque tights (to preserve what was left of the wearer's modesty). It was not a garment suitable for Sunday school, but more for hanging around in bus shelters smoking Gold Leaf. *Arctotis adpressa* 'Hayley' is one of those chirpy daisies that has the same innocent but knowing attitude – nothing too explicit, but just enough to thrill.

From slightly silvered, crispy-looking foliage emerge 40cm (16in) long skinny stems. On top of these, gathered around a yellow-speckled central boss, are flowers the colour of fine-cut marmalade with petals flaring outwards and upwards in a pleasantly flirtatious manner.

This is a great plant for containers. For the strongest plants, sow seed in autumn and overwinter under glass. Prick out from seed trays straight into 8cm (3½in) pots to avoid causing additional disturbance.

Tickseed
Coreopsis grandiflora 'Rising Sun'

Long-flowering, hardy perennial for borders and beds

Flowering time: June–October

Coreopsis grandiflora 'Rising Sun' is a prairie plant from North America, where it grows amongst the wide-open grassland where 'the buffalo roam and the deer and the antelope play' (and, if you believe the lyrics of Dr Brewster Higley, 'where never is heard a discouraging word, and the sky is not clouded all day').

The flowers are pretty, semi-double yellow daisies that look as if they have been attacked by a scissor-wielding lunatic – every petal is tattered and uneven like Robinson Crusoe's trousers. In the centre is a reddish splodge the colour of dropped jam. It is a strong-growing plant about 50cm (20in) tall that looks great against dark-leaved shrubs and interplanted with waving grass (to echo its native habitat).

Sow seed in its flowering position any time between April and June (after the last frost). Keep a sharp lookout for slugs and, if necessary, use copper bands around the seedlings, which can be a good deterrent.

Dahlia
Dahlia 'Clarion'

Beautifully simple, custard-yellow, tender perennial

Flowering time: July–September

There is a moment in about May when one is sick and tired of yellow: we have had thousands of daffodils (the year's first proper splash of colour) and the insistent yellow of forsythia. After a month of this, you can feel desperate for more subtle colours. However, even tasteful pink and baby blue can pall, so by the end of July you find yourself hankering for a bit of brash. That is what dahlias were born for: they were never intended to be subtle and this irrepressibly cheerful specimen is no exception. Growing *Dahlia* 'Clarion' is like having Little Richard dancing in your border after a month of serenely beautiful Bach cantatas.

Dahlias grow from collected seed but they will not come true to the parent this way. Every seed has the potential, but you could instead discover a completely different and wonderful dahlia that you could name after yourself.

Daffodil
Narcissus 'Bunting'

A very perky, bi-coloured daffodil for a border or naturalising

Flowering time: April

Spring just would not be spring without skipping lambs, soft green leaves, a plague of hungry baby rabbits, the first aphids and, of course, daffodils. They are the first heralds of a new season: no longer is the country bathed in beige for stronger colours are coming back into our lives. This is the first brashness of the year. There is little subtlety in a daffodil: this one is like a lemon ice cream with an orange centre, having plenty of zest and ping. It is a Division 7 (Jonquilla) narcissus, which means that it is sweetly scented and carries more than one flower per stem.

Plant bulbs in autumn at one and a half times their own depth (deeper if naturalising in grass). These narcissi flower best in full sun in drier soils. Propagate from offsets.

Waterlily
Nymphaea 'Pygmaea Helvola'

A miniature waterlily, perfect for even the smallest pond

Flowering time: June–September

Not everybody has room for a pond: for the vast majority of people the idea of reproducing Monet's garden at Giverny is an unfulfillable dream. However, almost everybody has room for a half-barrel and even in that this little waterlily will happily thrive.

All *Nymphaea* 'Pygmaea Helvola' needs is about 30cm (12in) of water and it will only spread about 60cm (2ft). In return it will provide you with buttery-yellow, star-shaped flowers and shiny green leaves mottled with bronze – the colour of a stuffed olive. Teamed with a miniature rush (*Typha*), a small pond will attract all sorts of wildlife, including frogs (provided they have some sort of access ramp), dragonflies and birds. In this way you can keep your wildest Jeremy Fisher fantasies alive.

Divide established plants in spring to maintain vigour. Propagate by separating rhizomes and potting on. Seed can be sown under glass in autumn, but be watchful as seedheads sink.

Cape figwort
Phygelius 'Candydrops Cream'

A perfect patio plant with soft, buttery-yellow flowers

Flowering time: June–October

People are often put off by the idea of yellow flowers in their gardens. Daffodils are fine (because they are early and brighten up dull plots) but sunshine- and fried-egg yellow is banned. It can be rather a 'look at me, look at me' colour, but that is no reason to expunge it completely from your colour scheme.

Phygelius 'Candydrops Cream' bears the sort of gentle yellow that neither scares horses nor brings on fits among the sensitive. The clusters of jingling bells are much more the colour of pale school custard than sunflowers and sweetcorn. The Candydrops group (of which there are different colours) are bred to be much shorter than most phygelius, which are evergreen shrubs that reach about 1.5m (4ft) high.

These plants are specially developed for pots and hanging baskets, and are hardy and early flowering. They are best in sun or limited shade and will grow to about 45cm (18in) high with a spread of 30cm (12in). They make a good centrepiece in larger containers.

Tulip
Tulipa tarda

A small, but very early, species tulip

Flowering time: February–March

Tulips are usually presumed to be the show-offs of the bulb world. As erect as Prussian military attachés, they puff out their chests and stand proud as the spring unfurls around them. Not all are so brazen: there is a whole underworld of much smaller, more delicate and generally more modest tulips. These are usually the species tulips. Most of their bigger relations have been hybridised and refined over centuries, but the species can usually still be found happily growing wild out there on distant mountainsides. *Tulipa tarda* will often have two or three lemon-drizzled flowers on each stem. It is only a few centimetres high, but if it is happy it will bulk up merrily. It has a delicate, slightly peppery scent.

This tulip prefers a slightly peatier soil. Seed can be sown in a frame in autumn but may take from four to seven years to flower; it's much easier to take offsets and grow them on.

Pansy
Viola x *williamsii* 'Tiger Eyes'

Spectacular low-growing plant for pots or the edges of borders

Flowering time: all year round

Racehorses seldom win races by accident: success usually involves a lot of calculation, training and, in particular, breeding. Similar efforts are put into plant breeding, but presumably without so much galloping or profit for bookmakers. With plants, as with horses, many of the breeders' efforts will never fulfill their potential, and only the very few will win the Grand National.

This little plant, *Viola* x *williamsii* 'Tiger Eyes', has both form and staying power. The combination of pure gold traced with intricate tributaries of black is very effective. Even better, it can be grown as both winter or summer bedding, and looks best in containers.

Sow seed in either late winter (for summer displays) or in early autumn (for winter containers). Germination will take about three weeks. Harden off and plant out when large enough.

Zinnia

Zinnia haageana 'Aztec Sunset'

A short, multi-branched annual with bags of attitude

Flowering time: July–October

Rumba. The humid Cuban darkness, the fluttering of moths, the scent of gardenia and cigar smoke, the tang of sweat and the brutal rhythm of the night. *Zinnia haageana* 'Aztec Sunset' looks like the ruffled sleeves of a twinkle-toed maracas player. There are almost more frilled petals than strictly necessary, which can look a little ridiculous, but the flowers still look both impressive and exotic. Even more extraordinary, all this flamboyance and strutting is compressed into a plant that is seldom more than 15cm (6in) high.
Be aware, however, that not every flower will be this colour: some will be red, some orange and some pale yellow. It is like having a lottery ticket in every seed packet.

Can be sown as early as February, provided you can maintain a steady temperature of about 20°C (68°F), and as late as April. This variety is very mildew resistant.

ndex

Picture credits

BBC Books and *Gardeners' World Magazine* would like to thank the following for providing photographs. While every effort has been made to trace and acknowledge all photographers, we should like to apologize should there be any errors or omissions.

Peter Anderson p183; Torie Chugg p21, p29, p91; Ray Cox p85, p141; Sarah Cuttle p33, p95, p163, p205; Paul Debois p49, p83, p109, p137, p145, p151, p179, p191; Melanie Eclare p201; *Gardeners' World Magazine* p139, p159; Neil Holmes p115; Caroline Hughes p51, p99; Jason Ingram p25, p31, p37, p39, p43, p47, p59, p61, p63, p67, p79, p87, p89, p93, p105, p111, p113, p121, p125, p127, p131, p133, p147, p149, p165, p167, p171, p189, p203; Lynn Keddie p15, p207; Dianna Jazwinski p103, p195; David Murray p57, p71, p101, p169, p177, p193; Howard Rice p129, p173, p197; Sabina Ruber p65, p175; Tim Sandall p13, p17, p19, p41, p45, p53, p73, p81, p107, p119, p135, p153, p155, p161, p181, p209, p211; William Shaw p11, p55, p75, p77, p123, p143, p185, p199; John Trenholm p23, p27, p35, p117, p157, p187; Mark Winwood p69; Jo Whitworth p97